The Day I Found
The LORD
(For Myself)

The Day I Found
The LORD
(For Myself)

By

LINDA ROSE-CROSBY

ReadersMagnet, LLC

The Day I Found The LORD (For Myself)
Copyright © 2024 by Linda Rose-Crosby

Published in the United States of America

Library of Congress Control Number: 2024900471

ISBN   Paperback: 979-8-89091-447-7
ISBN   eBook: 979-8-89091-448-4

All rights reserved. No part of this publication may be reproduced, stored in a retrieval system or transmitted in any way by any means, electronic, mechanical, photocopy, recording or otherwise without the prior permission of the author except as provided by USA copyright law.

The opinions expressed by the author are not necessarily those of ReadersMagnet, LLC.

ReadersMagnet, LLC
10620 Treena Street, Suite 230 | San Diego, California, 92131 USA
1.619. 354. 2643 | www.readersmagnet.com

Book design copyright © 2023 by ReadersMagnet, LLC. All rights reserved.

Cover design by Jhie Oraiz
Interior design by Dorothy Lee

DEDICATION

This book is dedicated to Myself, Linda Rose-Crosby, (Buffy/Sweet Baby) For the commitment I made to God.

There is therefore now no condemnation to them which are in Christ Jesus, who walk not after the flesh, but after the Spirit. (Romans 8:1 KJV)

THANK YOU

To my husband,

Roy Harrison Crosby, (Sweet Baby)

For accepting me, for who I was, for who I became, For who I am.

So ought men to love their wives as their own bodies. He that loveth his wife loveth himself. For no man ever yet hated his own flesh; but nourisheth and cherisheth it, even as the Lord the church. (Ephesians 5:28-29 KJV)

SPECIAL ACKNOWLEDGMENT

All the glory belongs to God!

TABLE OF CONTENTS

Dedication 5
Thank You 7
Special Acknowledgment 9
Prologue 13
The Early Years 15
Rebellion 19
In The Army Now 21
Texas, My Home 26
South Carolina Bound 29
Georgia Blues 31
Carolina Sunshine 33
My Godsend, My Husband 37
The Day I Found The LORD (For Myself) 43
Personal Viewpoints 45
Linda's Prayer: 48
Sickness 49
Epilogue 51
Resources And References 59

PROLOGUE

For a very long time, the LORD has been my shepherd. There were days when I could not see my way through. He rescued me from the valleys, lifted me to the hills, and placed me on the mountaintop.

When I look back over my life living outside the Ark of Safety, Jesus Christ, I could not have made it without Him watching over me. And the prayers of my mama.

He sent me an amazing man, who became my boyfriend and is now my husband. A wonderful human being that I can always lean on, and will do anything in his own power for me.

The LORD allowed me to be who I was and who I became and who I am.

I am eternally grateful that the LORD has smiled on me.

THE EARLY YEARS

My relationship with the LORD began at an early age.

My mama and my second oldest sister, who also was like a mama to me, instilled God in me. Both of them have passed on. God rest their souls. I always saw my mama praying, lifting up holy hands, and looking toward Heaven. And she would shed a few tears. Now, you talking about faith without wavering, Mrs. Katie had it. Her real name was Kate, but when I was a little girl, mama and I would often take a slow walk downtown, because mama never learned how to drive. We shopped at stores where she had credit on trust, by word of mouth that she would pay later. My mama came from very humble beginnings. You see, I am from the South, so the good white folks at the stores where we frequented called her Mrs. Katie.

What I am about to say may be offensive to some, but not to me because I know what, I am. As I mentioned, my mama and I used to walk downtown. Well, on this particular day, we went to buy me some shoes. You see, my mama could not afford to buy new shoes so we went to a second-hand store. When we arrived there, I was very tired and my feet were hurting because we had walked about a mile. I had outgrown my shoes, and they had a hole in the sole. Now, let me take a minute to explain. Back then black folks were not allowed to sit down in the good white folks' stores. I was tired, I sat down. There was a little white girl and her mama in the store. The little white girl said to her mama, "Mama, mama, look at that n****r, sitting down." But I did not get up until my mama told me to. This was during the times when our town had water fountains that said, "Whites Only, and Colored." Every time I tried to drink from the other race's fountain, my mama would stopped me. So, one day, I asked the white lady behind the counter, "Why Not?" and my mama told me to shut my mouth. Those were just two incidents out of the many that I wanted to add.

My mama was a sweet, and gentle soul, filled with the Holy Spirit of God. She had an old ragged white Holy Bible that she read from teaching about His Word. The Bible had pictures of God, Jesus Christ, and his disciples. I especially remember the pictures of little children sitting at the LORD'S feet. The Scripture that left an imprint on my life was: "Suffer the little children to come unto me, and forbid them not: for of such is the kingdom of God."

(Mark 10:14 KJV)

When I was a little girl, I lived in the country on a farm, because my daddy was a farmer for a rich old white man, and we worked mainly in tobacco for him. My mama never worked on the farm. She lived in town, and I lived with both of them at alternate times. There was a lady living on the farm who chawed on chewing tobacco. I was curious, so I stole a piece of hers. When I began chewing it, I swallowed the juice, which made me very sick to my stomach. Lying on the grass, I looked at the sky and prayed. That was my first and last time trying to chew tobacco. My daddy's mama dipped snuff, and so did one of her daughters. I am glad I never picked up any of those habits.

When we lived in Winston Salem, NC, on the top floor of an apartment, my youngest brother, Joe, and I spat down from a balcony on a couple walking on the street. The lady thought it was her companion; they started fighting. We ran and hid. My brother and I were very devilish growing up because he thought everything was a joke. I was his trusted sidekick. Where he led, I was there as well.

While my family and I lived in Olanta, SC my brother, Joe, and I used to look down into a big ditch. That is where a water moccasin snake (also called a cottonmouth because the inside of its mouth is white) lived. We would wait for it to surface, and then we would run away. Sometimes, we threw rocks, sticks, or whatever at it. One time we saw a great big turtle, in the ditch as well.

I was a tomboy, I shot marbles, climbed trees, etc. Once, I fell out of a tree and busted my forehead. I have the scars to take to my grave. But my favorite times were playing hopscotch, jacks, jumping rope, and bike riding. I never could double Dutch though, but was great at Hula-hooping, and with a footsy toy. During this time, my brother, Joe, and I also played games with our nephews, our second oldest sister's sons; the first, second, and third oldest, respectively.

In the late 1960s, my mama bought me a black life-size doll baby. I remember what she looks like to this very day. Tall, dark-complexioned, brown eyes, black hair with a white hair bow, rose chambray dress, and white Mary Jane shoes. Her beautiful long legs were endless.

Sometimes, I now look back over my life and wish I had been more appreciative of things that I no longer have. But oh, well, we live and accept.

In elementary school, I wanted my name Linda to be spelled with a y instead of an i, so I changed it on my own. I was so headstrong until I even changed my last name from Rose to Rhodes. In junior high school, I got into a fight with a girl, and she said, "I'm going to call the police." So, I yelled, "The police ain't nothing but a man with a badge and a gun. Call him." As a young girl, I was fearless; authority figures meant nothing to me.

I do not know why I did those things. Looking back now, I guess I just wanted to do them. My rebellion started early. As I am lying in bed, thinking back on childhood memories, there are so many.

THE DAY I FOUND THE LORD (FOR MYSELF)

One of my favorite memories is of my royal blue dress that fell just below my knees. It had one gold stripe on each side. I can still see the shiny gold buttons on both sides that ran from my shoulders down to my knees. I always wore that dress with navy blue nylon stockings with seams on the back. My seams had to be perfect on my calves. I was fanatical about that one detail. I stood in front of the mirror until they were exactly like I needed them to be. It did not matter how long it took.

My desire to have everything perfect, many times, caused me to be the last one out of the house for church. I can still hear my brother honking the horn, and yelling, "We're going to be late for church, Kate's baby, hurry up." I am the baby of my siblings and make no mistake, I was my mama's baby indeed.

When I lived with my second oldest sister, her husband, and their seven children, she was like a mama to me, too. I was more of a sister to my nephews and nieces than their aunt.

My second oldest sister loved gospel music. She always played different gospel albums, but her favorites were Shirley Caesar and Mahalia Jackson. She named one of her daughters Mahalia.

On Sundays, we attended service at our family church. And during the week, I was always in the presence of an evangelist and elders at different churches. My sister had a favorite evangelist that she followed everywhere. Later on, her husband started singing with a gospel group. I was always at various gospel programs as well; then after the programs, we went home and ate. We stayed up late at night watching different evangelists on television. For me, there was no escaping the LORD.

REBELLION

When I came of age, I took a different path. An ungodly one. I guess you can say I strayed off of the path. I put my religion on a shelf. It was time to break free, so I did. If only I knew what was to become of me, I would have done so many things differently.

I started going to house parties where my friends' parents were not strict with them. There were no father figures in the homes. Sex talk? What was that? No one ever sat me down and talked about sex. I remember hearing, "Don't let the little boys fool you. They only want one thing." I believe my role models were too embarrassed to talk about sex with me. After my first marriage, I shared some things with mama, and she could not believe them. Many years later, I discovered what I heard concerning little boys to be true.

When I was in school, our teachers showed us sex education films about venereal diseases. They were so gross that I did not want to look. But I felt like I had to see what was going on, so I peeped through my fingers, but I missed a lot of what they said.

After school, I would put my books down and head straight to a neighborhood nightclub, where everyone knew me as Baby Linda. I wanted to practice my dance moves before the party began. One time, I did a dance move and split the back of my pants wide open but kept right on dancing. I was a dancing fool. My mama did not approve of my nightclubbing, so my fourth oldest sister and I would sneak out of the house. Sometimes, we found ourselves fifteen miles away in another town.

Growing up, my friends and I walked up and down the main strip, Highway 52, in my hometown of Lake City, SC. Long before social media, the main strip was the place to be if you were looking for someone you had not seen in a while. One time I wanted to see this guy who I had not seen for a long time. Finally, I saw him but did not get the reaction I was expecting. When he saw me, he yelled out of his car, calling me fat, and drove away in a hurry. I was heartbroken because I was only weighing 139 pounds and thought I was fine.

At that very moment, I became conscious of my weight and have been ever since.

Today, his actions would be called body shaming.

I lived with my oldest brother, his wife, and their two children for a while. I was the babysitter for my nephew and niece. My brother also had an older daughter years before.

Before my second oldest brother got remarried, I lived with him for a while, too.

I am part of an enormous family, especially on Mrs. Katie's side. I have many nephews, nieces, cousins, etc. When the Holy Bible said to be fruitful and multiply, my family did not waste a moment. And they are still multiplying.

God never blessed me to carry a baby to term. I had female reproductive problems, but do not cry for me, for I had my furbaby, beloved Belle, (Princess), and now I have my furbaby, baby Bella.

IN THE ARMY NOW

When I was in the U.S. Army Basic Training, my platoon had to present a properly folded American flag to an official. I was chosen to give the flag to him. If you know anything about the military, when you present a flag, the only color that should be shown is the blue background with the white stars. Well, after I had presented it, I saw the color red, so I stepped out of formation and tried to tuck it in. I breached protocol, but no action was taken against me because I was a new recruit, and still learning about military life.

Also, I had to march in a big parade. I was so proud because there were dignitaries watching us. Then I heard "Eyes Right," the military way of saluting when marching.

I truly loved every military command given to us.

Being in the military was one of my greatest experiences.

While going through my Advanced Individual Training (AIT), I went to the bowling alley every night, except for one, because I was sick. My favorite snacks were pork skins, an orange soda, and pickled pig feet. The guy behind the counter always gave me free food and drink. It was more like being in college than the military. There was so much freedom. But the next morning it was back to soldiering.

For the first time since school, I did not have a boyfriend. Guys wanted to talk to me, but I was only interested in bowling. There was this one guy, a Black Puerto Rican. I had never heard of such a person, because where I came from, it was just blacks and whites. One girl wanted to fight me over him. I was not even interested in him. I set her straight and went about my business—bowling.

After finishing my Advanced Individual Training, I had a flight scheduled to go home. After that, I was to report to my Permanent Duty Station. But someone robbed me of all of my money. If you want to know what happened after that, read my first book titled *The Day My Life Changed: (An Accident Survivor)*.

Back to my forehead's scars, when I was in the U.S. Army, stationed in Texas, for my Permanent Duty. Shortly after I got there, one morning I went into the mess hall to eat, and I had to take my cap off (the cap is part of the uniform). And as I was going through the chow line, there were these two cooks serving food. When they saw me, one of them commented, "She is a good-looking girl, but her head is busted up." That is when I became conscious of my scars. From that day on, when I went to the hairdressers, I always told them no matter what style they gave me to cover my scars.

In the military, while stationed at my Permanent Duty Station in Texas, I literally took leave of all of my religious upbringing. No parental control at all. I started with the cigarettes and the mixed drinks. And oh, my goodness, so many guys wanted to talk to me. Yes, I had boyfriends in junior high and high school, but not like this. I could take my pick. Even though I left two boyfriends behind, one of them wanted to marry me. The other one was a guy I met at a nightclub. Eventually, I forgot about both of them and started seeing someone else.

The soldiers spoiled me to the core, because what the military did not provide for me; they did. I got engaged to be married twice. My first fiancé got shipped to Korea. At first, I missed him very much. That was a very sad time in my life. He introduced me to Teddy Pendergrass's music. We sat around, ate, smoked cigarettes, and drank mixed drinks. Sometimes, he drank stronger stuff while listening to Teddy Pendergrass, "Close The Door." I really and truly had a marvelous time with this man. He was my first really intimate boyfriend. If you know what I mean.

But time marched on, and I met someone else, but my fiancé was still sending me money to build toward our future together. By the time he got back from Korea, I had run through all the money, and we went our separate ways. But it was hard.

My second fiancé, while he was on the Army Post with me, everything was fine, but his enlistment ended. He still wanted to marry me, so we continued with our long-distance relationship. Our relationship was like a dream that I did not want to wake up from. I will never forget how romantic it can be, with the only light in the room coming from a huge fish aquarium. The aquarium was a vibrant display of colors, with fish in shades of blue, green, orange, black and more, each in unique shapes and sizes. The soft music playing in the background added the perfect touch. I met his brother and sister-in-law because they were also stationed in Texas.

My fiancé was from Alabama and wanted me to meet his sisters also. I took a trip there and went shopping with them. That was the first time I discovered people cooked rice with sugar—I did not like it—I was used to rice being cooked with salt. Later, he came back to the Army Post, so we could get blood tests and go to the courthouse to get married. When we got to the courthouse, I could not move. My hand would not open the door. We sat in the car and talked for a long time. I was shuddering to no end, got sick to my stomach, and broke out in a full-blown cold sweat. The next thing I knew, I was on a flight headed to SC.

I went home for a few days, got myself together, then headed back to Texas. I still have a beautiful picture of his brother, his brother's wife, and their baby daughter. I also have a picture of his sister-in-law and me while she was pregnant. We were close friends, and I was at their home more than on the Post.

All of them were fantastic people.

THE DAY I FOUND THE LORD (FOR MYSELF)

After that relationship ended, I met someone else. If you believe in karma or whatever—you will get enjoyment out of this—he left me for someone else. But while we were together, he took me to a beautiful city in Texas, called Corpus Christi. We went to a lake where the water was crystal clear, bluish-green, and cool. Wow! What a beautiful time it was. There I saw so many people dressed in multi-colored outfits for the occasion, scattered along the water's edge. He had a sports car, and we took a trip to visit some of his family members. At night, I slept on a top bunk bed for the first time and spent the entire night lying in one position, praying, and looking at the ceiling. This was the only way I knew to keep from falling over the edge. I was happy to get back to the Army Post.

When I was living on the Post, I had a roommate. She always called me Duchess. Why? I do not know. She wrote me a letter saying how happy she was about being a friend of mine, and I still have it to this very day.

I only had a few close friends on the Post, but on the outskirts of Killeen, Texas; I had a crew that I used to visit. We always had a blast. My main friend was a government service (GS) worker who operated computers with me when I worked at Cold Storage. While at my Permanent Duty Station, I worked at Cold Storage and Dry Storage.

Also, right outside the Post, the city bus ran, and I used to make a run for the border. This is where I ate so many enchiladas. I was introduced to a drink called the Suicide. A mixture of two different drinks, (kind of tart), but very refreshing. There was a restaurant miles from the Post that served barbecue roast beef. The first time, I borrowed my friend, the GS worker's car, I went to the restaurant. After I got my food and was ready to head back, the car would not start. I called my friend, and she told me what had to be done. Now, this is crazy but true. In order for the car to crank, you had to press down on the hood on the driver's side and shake it. The gear kept getting stuck, and this was the remedy. And it worked. I had to have a guy from the restaurant come out and help because I was not strong enough. Another favorite of mine was red rice and sausage. I had to drive even farther to another restaurant for that.

When I was in the military service, one time I came home for a visit. On this trip, when I got to Atlanta, GA, I had a stopover and had to switch planes. The flight I switched over to had a little white girl traveling to NC sitting behind me. She was very talkative and kept asking me to guess her name. Now, before I go any further, I would like to say my oldest sister and her family settled in NC. She has passed on; God rest her soul. Her children are still there. To make my point, North Carolinians have a more pronounced accent than South Carolinians.

During Basic Training, one of my friends was from Germany, and she used to tease me all the time, when I said, Oh, Lord, she spelled it, "Oh, Lawd."

I call the North Carolinian accent tangy. Well, the little girl kept saying to me, "I bet you can't guess my name." Her voice alone was killing me. Then she said, "It's a candy bar." So, I began calling out different candies' names. I know it had to be about half an hour or more. After conversing and guessing, I finally gave up. Then she said, "My name is Heath." That was my first time hearing of such a candy bar. I said to myself, "Why is this child flying alone?" I just wanted to end that harrowing plane ride. Of course, I met all kinds of people on different flights.

TEXAS, MY HOME

The Army gave me an opportunity to go to Hawaii for six months, to see if I wanted to further my military career because my enlistment was ending. Mrs. Katie wanted me to come home, so that was the end of my military life. But I was not ready to leave my partying ways behind yet. I became a resident of Texas. I loved Texas. My friend, who called me Duchess, and I rented an apartment together, because she was like a sister to me. There was a food home delivery truck that came right to my front door. I had an account where I could purchase my meat, milk, eggs, butter, etc., and pay later. I only went to the grocery store for vegetables and grains, or other items I needed.

While living in Texas, I went to this humongous indoor flea market. The sheer number of vendors selling their wares amazed me. My mind was racing. I did not know which one to go to first. And because of the competition, the prices were a steal. By the time I left out of there, I had a little of this and a little of that. I did not know where I was going to put all of that stuff. Some of it, I still have to this very day.

During this period, I had a fascination with snakes. On my way out of the flea market, heading to the parking lot, there was a snake vendor at the entrance. I stopped there. Amazed at what I saw. There were so many kinds and colors of giant snakes. I was too shocked to be afraid. My feet would not move, and my eyes were going here and there. I said to myself, "If my mama could see me now, she would not believe it." Because I am desperately afraid of worms, and here I was looking at giant snakes. Mind-blowing.

When I was growing up, I worked in tobacco. We planted, topped, cropped, and stringed tobacco. I work at the barns, and on a harvester machine in the fields.

Have you ever seen a tobacco worm?

Just thinking about it gives me jitters.

When I was younger, and I saw one, it stopped me dead in my tracks. I could not work after that. It was the end of my workday; my daddy would give me permission to go and play. As I got older, I had to walk away and return to work. Being daddy's little girl did not work for me anymore. While I was working at the barn and saw a worm, my daddy gave me minutes to collect myself, then began working, again. In the fields on the harvester machine, I took a deep breath and continued working. I needed the money for clothes, books, and school supplies. That desire or need enticed me to keep working. Disregarding the worms, I kept pressing on. But I am still frightened of all kinds of worms to this very day.

My second oldest sister summoned me home, because my mama wanted me to come back home; she could not bear having me away any longer, so I moved back to SC.

My friend, the one that called me Duchess, stayed at the apartment until she got shipped overseas. Then, years later, I received a letter and a picture of her and a guy she met. I have it to this very day as well. God bless her wherever she may be.

After leaving Texas, I traveled home to SC on a Trailways bus. There was a guy that got on the bus in Meridian, MS. He tried to get my phone number and he bugged me all the way from MS to Florence, SC. When the bus pulled into the station, and the bus driver opened the door for me to get off, there was my mama standing there. The bus driver said to the guy, "I bet you will leave her alone now because there is her mama." I was surprised because I did not know he was aware of my agony. During my travels while in the military service, I met many characters. I say characters because in this thing we call life; we are in a production on the stage, playing different parts—regardless.

SOUTH CAROLINA BOUND

After moving back home, I put my military skills to work by working for different computer companies. I worked Monday through Friday. On Friday through Sunday, I went to nightclubs. One particular night, I was at one of my frequent clubbing spots. A guy approached me while I was sitting at the bar. I was not interested in him. Lo-and-behold, I saw someone from my past. So, to get the other guy to leave me alone, I asked this guy to pretend like he was my boyfriend. And it worked. But it worked too well, and we ended up spending twelve years together.

Out of all those years, only one of them was good, and that was the first year. But over the years, we used to go to this beautiful water spot in Timmonsville, SC where the water was green, and so clear, you could see different kinds of fish swimming around. We would drink wine coolers together. I often thought I could reach in and grab a fish with my hand. The place was kind of secluded. But there were a few people there as well, fishing on the bank of the lake. Those were great times.

A few months later, one of my brothers got killed by a train, God rest his soul, so I am desperately afraid of trains. I remember one time; when I came to the same railroad tracks where my brother got hit. The crossing gates were down, but I said to myself, I can make it before the train gets to the crossing. I proceeded onto the tracks and when I looked to the right, there was the train right upon me. The light shone brightly into my face. So, I panicked, threw my car into reverse; slid over to the passenger side, opened the door, got out, and started peeing. I did not care who saw me, and I did not even look to see if anything was behind me when I threw my car into reverse. The following Sunday, I went to church and told my testimony, and shouted and danced all over the church. I was grateful to be alive.

As far as the military goes, I was a forerunner because I was the first of my family members to enlist in the service. And I was the first female in my family that started smoking cigarettes. My second oldest sister was so disappointed in me for doing so. She used to say to me: "Linda, take that cigarette out of your mouth. It looks so bad for a girl to be smoking." I laughed at myself sometimes—look who's smoking—church girl.

After I had been out of the service for a while, I decided I wanted to go back in. I had to take the physical exam again. My results showed I had Mitral Valve Prolapse, meaning one of my heart valves would not open or close properly. It has been a long time now, so I cannot remember which one is defective. Then I asked the doctor what could be done. He said to me, "Nothing," so I asked him what can I do. He said, "Grit your teeth and bear it."

Over the years, for some relationships, I had to do the same thing. I am still doing the same for some now. Ha-ha! Just kidding.

GEORGIA BLUES

There was a point in my life when I was living in Atlanta, Georgia (1986), and I was homeless. I was living out of my car. Each morning, I went to a convenience store to wash up and get ready for work. Every morning, the clerk at the store gave me a free cup of hot coffee and the key to the bathroom. Once I got dressed, I stayed around and talked until it was time for me to go to work. No one was the wiser at the furniture store where I was working.

I got back on my feet somewhat, and rented an apartment in a ritzy area. I did not have a bed to sleep in or furniture to sit on. And most of the time, I was hungry. There was a convenience store, not the one mentioned above, where I would go and steal candy bars. I did not have the money to pay for them. When things got better for me, I went back to that same store and tried to pay the manager for the stolen candy, but he would not take the money. He said to me, "I knew you were stealing all along."

Things back then were rough, but God brought me through all of them. Even though I was living in Georgia, I did not change my driver's license, because I have always considered myself a resident of South Carolina. This is my home, the only place where I want to be.

Now, to this very day, I do not waste a morsel of food because I know what it is like for people who are starving. I thank God every day for a roof over my head and the food on my table. But during those bad times, I dressed to perfection, that is why no one was the wiser. My mama brought me up to believe that no one knows your business unless you tell them.

If you are wondering, how did I get myself into that mess of a situation? It is called stupidity. During that time, God stepped in and saved me from me. Because I was in love with a man more than I was with myself. I would have done anything to please him in those days. He moved to Georgia, so I quit my job to follow him. That was one of the worst mistakes I had ever made. But as it goes, love makes you do crazy things. After that, I learned the meaning of self-preservation, and before you can love someone else, you must love yourself.

CAROLINA SUNSHINE

I always thought I had to wear makeup, especially lipstick because I always felt naked without it. One day, I had my face professionally made up for the first time. It was at the mall in Florence, SC. I stood at the makeup counter and a young lady behind the counter did my makeover. I was so impressed with the change until I bought everything in that line of makeup. When I left the mall, I went home then went to Walmart, and pranced around in there. I wanted everyone to see how good I looked.

From then on, I wore makeup until the coronavirus hit in 2020. But the whole time I wore it, my face did not once break out. I still cannot figure that out, because I have very sensitive skin. Oh, well.

My hair has always looked good. At first, I had long hair but in 1990; I got it cut. After the death of my mama, I was looking for a way to keep my spirits from sinking, so I thought a new hairstyle might do me some good. One of my nieces told me about a fabulous hairdresser. I went to her and the rest is history because she is still my hairdresser to this very day. She is also one of my best friends. Although retired, she still does my hair. I am so blessed to have her as a loyal friend.

Today my hair is long again, and I like it that way, and I plan to never get it cut again.

While living with my daddy to take care of him, and the twins of my fourth oldest sister, because he was so distraught after the passing of my mama, on May 2, 1990. Out of the blue, one day I caught bronchitis. It made me so sick that I lost my taste for smoking. My second oldest sister was glad that my smoking days were over. I was still married to my first husband, but we were separated. After that period of living with my daddy and the twins was over, I purchased my first home in December 1994. Can you say freedom? I was ecstatic. Just in time for Christmas, my favorite time of the year—Jesus Christ's Birthday.

My first husband was the guy I met at the nightclub and left behind when I went into the military. From that relationship, I learned how to never backtrack. Because we separated and got back together so many times until it was ridiculous. The only way I survived that marriage was to take my religion back off the shelf. The reason I stayed in it for so long was because of my position in the church, and I thought it was the godly thing to do. I was miserable. Then came the year 1995. I just could not take it any longer. I had to go. I started planning how to make my escape. Each morning when I went to work, I took a little of my belongings out of the house at a time. I stored them at a friend's house. Before I knew it, I had everything that I did not want to leave behind. At least everything that I could carry. I still wanted my first-floor model television. I loved that TV. The only way I could get it after I left was to pay him a large sum of money. He knew how much I loved that thing, so he capitalized on it. That should give you a general idea of what my first marriage was like.

In the beginning, oh, I thought the sun had risen and shone on him. Believe it or not, I thought he was a godsend, because I had just gotten out of the military, and was back home and living on my own. I prayed for God to send me someone; so be careful what you pray for.

I considered my marriage to be over from my perspective, even though I was not divorced yet.

During my military days, I loved to take pictures. Shortly after I had gotten settled into my new home, I was going through some old stuff, and I ran across my photo albums from back then, and loose pictures of my military times. I also found a camera that belonged to my fiancé, who was from Alabama. I felt tempted to develop the film, but the thought of revisiting both the happy and painful memories made me scared. I tossed the film and the camera in the trash. And everything that I found relating to my first husband, I did the same—No backtracking.

I still have pictures of some of those military times to take me back and bring a smile. God blessed me to have met some of the kindest, sweetest, caring, and genuine military officers, sergeants, and enlisted persons in my life. I am forever grateful.

Thank God, I am still living in my home.

Once again, I put my religion back on a shelf. You can guess what happened next. I started seeing someone else. By this time, I had enough of black men. I wanted something different, a white man. I soon found out a man is a man. But the white man taught me that just because you are the boss on a job does not mean that you cannot work right alongside your workers. Being with him is where my love of coffee came from, because he bought me a cup of hot coffee every morning. He was a really nice guy, but our different skin colors got in the way. He left me for someone who looked more like him.

Then, I got a job in the hospitality industry in Myrtle Beach, SC. And of course, you know what happened. I met someone. For our first date, he asked me to meet him at a restaurant that I was not comfortable with, but he loved the food there. I agreed to meet him. I started staying in a condominium on the beach more than at home. By this time, remember, I had already purchased my home. This is where my love of Chinese food became an obsession. He would order all kinds of different dishes, and I ate until my belly and heart were content. But the really good part is I did not gain any weight. He had a convertible car. On one occasion we went from Myrtle Beach, SC to Wilmington, NC with the top down. Our destination was to a restaurant on the pier. The food was delicious, soft music was playing in the background, and the waves were crashing against the shore. The birds were chirping in the air. I closed my eyes, and all was right with the world. He expressed his desire to marry me, but I explained I was not yet divorced.

The year was 1997; the day was a Sunday. I was supposed to meet him and his family at a restaurant in Myrtle Beach, SC; but I did not show up. First, let me explain what my Sunday afternoons were like back then. Jazz music was my pleasure. Every Sunday afternoon, I would turn the radio on and let it soak into my spirit. My favorite place to sit and listen to it was at the foot of my bed in front of my bureau. Why there? That is where I kept my mail in a bottom drawer. And on Sundays, I cleaned it out while listening to Jazz. And to be honest, I loved sitting on the floor. Yes, I had furniture. The next day, I faced him. Shortly after that, I found a job closer to home. He was still living on the beach, so we grew apart.

MY GODSEND, MY HUSBAND

Need I tell you what happened next? I met my second husband, Roy H. Crosby, his nickname is Sweet Baby, in 1998. The best thing that ever happened to me was accepting Jesus Christ as my personal Savior. He is the second-best thing. When I met Sweet Baby, I told him I was a church girl with some secrets. I thank God, that Roy, gave me a chance for me to know the real me. By this, I mean loving myself more, and changing the way I think of myself with a new and improved mindset. And being a good enough human being.

One day, without warning, my former boyfriend from Myrtle Beach tried to come back into my life. I was not married to Sweet Baby yet. He even offered to take Sweet Baby and me out to eat, but I declined. Remember, I told you; I have learned my lesson about backtracking.

Sweet Baby was a police officer. Shortly after we met, he took a break from the police force and started driving over-the-road trucks transporting hazardous materials. I quit my job and joined him. We have had some amazing adventures, seen sights, and heard sounds that were spectacular. I do not drink liquor, but I have a shot glass from every state that we visited.

After I quit my job to go trucking with Sweet Baby, we caught a Greyhound bus from South Carolina to pick up a truck in Tennessee. Along the way, we had to switch buses. As we were leaving the bus station in Atlanta, GA, on a day that I was thankful to have on a winter coat, and floppy hat, as I was looking out the window with the raindrops drizzling down there were so many people sleeping on the street covered with cardboard boxes.

I just had to hold back the tears because many years ago, that could have been me. But the kindness of strangers kept me going. That is why, to this very day, if I can help someone, I do so without hesitation.

On one of our truck driving trips, we were heading to Canada. There was a steep bridge, and if Sweet Baby had not shifted into the right gear, we would have rolled backward. The silence was deafening. When we got to the border, an officer made us get out of the truck, and he went inside and rummaged through our belongings. I had to straighten everything back up. I even had to leave my purse, and that rattled me because I had my valuables in it. What can I say? Foreign countries have their rules, too.

Speaking of foreign countries, Sweet Baby and I took a Royal Caribbean Cruise in 1998, and when we returned to Florida; I thought we would never get off of that ship. The customs officials were very slow. That was my first and last cruise.

Being with Sweet Baby, I discovered the first of many good, and exciting things.

Getting back to our trucking days; the company paid Sweet Baby a certain number of cents per mile. We were out there to make dollars. There were only a few stops in between. So, when I had to use the bathroom, we had a makeshift toilet for me. I was like a cat marking my territory. I believe I marked every state that we traveled to. We now look back on that and laugh. Oh, but back then it was serious business.

At the truck stops, prostitution was rampant. One time we were at a truck stop trying to get some sleep and this happy harlot came knocking. She asked Sweet Baby if he need some company. He told her, "My company is right here with me, my wife." (Even though I was just his girlfriend.) She reluctantly left. Another time, Sweet

Baby was walking across a parking lot at a truck stop, and this wanton woman came up to him and grabbed him. I saw him pulled away and, knowing him like I do, he said nothing good to her. In truckers' language, they are called "lot lizards."

We were traveling, coming to this bridge that ran across the Louisiana Bayou, and suddenly, a 15-passenger white van stopped dead in its tracks right in front of us. Our vehicle was carrying a tank full of hazardous material. Sweet Baby slammed on the brakes and had to swerve to keep from crashing into the van. We almost jackknifed—where the cab and the trailer—link and form a 90-degree angle. V-shape. Then the driver of the van got out and went around to the passenger side of it, and just stood there. Sweet Baby got the steering of the truck back under control and we kept on trucking. Like I told you, we had to make dollars. God bless that poor fellow.

Well, after our trucking days were over, Sweet Baby bought a speedboat and named it Linda. In days long past, we would go to this river called Black River. He would put the boat into the water and after boating up and down the river, we would eat the lunch that he packed. Wow! Just speaking about it brings back amazing memories.

Why speak it? I am writing my second book, just like how I had to write my first book, by using a speech-to-write program because I cannot use my hands. I have bilateral carpal tunnel syndrome.

Also, in days long gone, God blessed us to have had a cabin cruiser, but that is another story. But I will say, we do not have either of them anymore because we are both permanently and totally disabled.

I remember when Sweet Baby and I had an above-the-ground huge swimming pool with a deck. For hours, I would lie on a floater in it. The sky was so blue and the trees were so green. The clouds were fluffy and the shape of them reminded me of different things. Just by admiring His creation, I felt closer to God. I got sunburned, but I did not mind. That is when I realized dark-skinned Black people can get sunburned, too. Was I living under a rock? Somehow, a hole got into our pool, and that was the end of my outdoor oneness with my Heavenly Father.

But it was a good thing, too, because all I wanted to do was lie in the pool. I lived for it. Sweet Baby would swim in the pool. I never learned how to swim, but that was okay. When I was in the military, I was told I had to learn to swim, but I was too afraid. My Sergeant did not press the issue, and I was happy. Sweet Baby got the pool fixed and gave it to a friend of ours.

I believe one reason I loved lying in the pool on the floater was that I enjoyed feeling the sun on my face.

The warmth of the sun makes me feel more alive than ever.

And have you guessed by now how much I find water to be soothing to my soul?

Even growing up working in the cotton, bean, and tobacco fields with the sun beaming down did not bother me. My problems were how long the rows were and when will I get to the end. And the critters that were lurking in the bushes.

The cotton was white and fluffy and the rows stretched seem like for miles. And one day, one of my sisters got stung by a cotton worm that was enclosed in the cotton boll. (A boll is shaped like a tiny football, in which moist fibers grow and push out from the newly formed seeds. As the boll ripens, it turns brown.) The cotton worm stung her in the face, causing her eyes to swell shut.

In the bean field, each day I had a quota for myself, because we got paid by the number of crates (a wooden crate with a lid). To reach my quota, sometimes, I would put the leaves off of the beans into the bottom and the middle of my crate to fill it. Because when I looked ahead at those long rows in front of me, it was just too much to bear and the only thing on my mind was getting to the end of them. There was an incident when someone put some bushes into their crate and a snake was found at the bottom when the crate was dumped.

Now, this was the worst for me, I was in the tobacco field working on a harvester machine, somehow, when the guy who was my cropper handed the tobacco leaves to me, a worm got on me. My job was to string the leaves manually. So, he said to me, "I love your pretty green necklace;" I said, I don't have on a necklace, then I started screaming, "Get it off of me!"

After having lunch under the shaded tree, I did not want to return to the fields, but I did not have any other choice. So, I did what I had to do—work—because I needed the money.

After those arduous days, I knew I wanted a job inside. I never wanted to have to work that hard again.

What was I thinking—I went into the military? Believe it or not, it was not hard for me at all. I even got an opportunity to eat at the officer's club.

Sweet Baby always says to me, "I don't know what military you were in, because I caught hell. When I was on bivouac, we had to stay out in the field many nights, eat with unwashed hands, low crawl through the mud, and do other kinds of military maneuvers."

Now, back to snakes. When I saw the giant snakes in Texas; I thought those were the biggest snakes I had ever seen. But many years later, after meeting Roy, I discovered he had a fascination with snakes, too. We used to watch programs about snakes on television. One day, I saw an anaconda on TV. Oh my God! Those snakes that I saw in Texas were babies compared to that thing. And we watched the movie "Anaconda," I could not sleep for days after seeing it. I am glad that my fascination with snakes is over because they are of the devil.

The court granted me a divorce in 2000.

THE DAY I FOUND THE LORD (FOR MYSELF)

There was a time when I trusted my life to no one but myself; then came Sweet Baby. He introduced me to a brand-new life and opened a door in my heart that I thought was closed forever. What a joy ride; Sweet Baby and I meeting at the same fork in the road. And traveling together ever since. I got remarried in 2001.

Two weeks after I got married, I called the Justice of the Peace and asked, "How can I get out of this?" Because I was frightened. A burnt child does not like the fire, and I was feeling the heat again.

Looking back, that would have been one of the worst mistakes I could have ever made.

I cannot describe or express how much my husband loves me. I have an older and wiser head now, so I know how to pursue things differently.

THE DAY I FOUND THE LORD
(For Myself)

The Day I Found The LORD (For Myself), I was suffering from debilitating pains for many years because of a horrific car accident. The pains were red-hot, and radiating like flames of a fire that was destroying everything in sight. Nothing could extinguish the raging inferno inside of me. I could not be touched because of the pressure points on my body. There were no relief from the twin torments, my mind and body. But I did not ask God why. I told Him, the pains let me know I am yet alive. By this time, my husband and I had separate bedrooms. While lying in bed and praying, I suddenly felt lifted out of the bed and taken up in a roaring wind. I heard voices I had never heard before. Fear took me over and I did not know what to do, so I prayed even harder and called on the name of Jesus Christ. When my body came back down, I felt different in my spirit. There was a calmness that I cannot explain even to this very day. And at that moment, I knew I had received the Gift of the Holy Spirit. The devil told me it was because I had just watched the movie, "King of Kings," about Jesus Christ the night before. But I did not listen to Satan because I knew he was a liar, and I had something he could not take away.

You see, the many years before I was living on the prayers of my mama. I grew up in the church, so I knew of the LORD, but I did not know Him. As I mentioned before, I put my religion on a shelf and took it off when I needed it. But after my transformation, I know now Who the LORD is, because I found Him for myself, and I pray now for myself and others.

When I was a young child, I experienced salvation, sanctification, and baptism, but I did not receive the gift of the Holy Spirit (Ghost) until that night. I was brought up saying the Holy Ghost. Now, I know the LORD, and his grace, mercy, truth, and lovingkindness. Even though I am saved by God's grace, sometimes without warning, fear still tries to creep into my heart. This used to be disconcerting to me, but not any longer. I now know that is a tactic of the enemy, the devil. He comes to control and conquer by planting seeds of doubt in your head. It is up to each person to not let the seeds of doubt grow by watering them. Because if you are not careful, he will have you second-guessing yourself about things that you should not even give a second thought. That is when prayer and the Holy Spirit make a difference in my life. I am a Christian and anointed by God. His Spirit dwells within me. God gives the anointing for all Christians. I give all of my thanks to God. My victory comes through my LORD and Savior, Jesus Christ. Everyone can experience the love and saving power of Jesus Christ.

You, too, can receive His love and saving power.

Satan, thought he had me,

God, reached down and grabbed me,

My life has never been the same since,

The Day I Found The LORD (For Myself).

PERSONAL VIEWPOINTS

These two things I find to be very profound:
There are people who talk to you when they find the time, and there are people who find the time to talk to you.

My friends, there is a major difference.

Be careful who you become acquainted with because some people can be toxic; and when they leave because you have had enough, they will fault you.

When it comes down to who I decide to be a friend to, I choose for myself. This I say, because some of my friends, most people, do not understand why they have become a friend of mine. Some people think I am too trusting. Maybe that is true, but until I see it differently, there is no need to talk to me about it. Because it goes in and out until my friend shows me they are not to be trusted. When they do, my eyes and ears are on them. In the future, I will be careful about what they say and what I say to them. And I say to myself, *I see you, now*.

There comes a time in each person's life when things become so clear and it is up to each individual to continue on the same path or take a different one.

From my personal experience, I have learned to take a different path because going the same way can only lead to destruction.

It is not an easy thing to do, but sometimes it is the best thing for you and them.

Crucial decisions are not to be taken lightly; weigh them out from every angle. Because you can only look the other way for so long, and then you have to face it. Things are not always what they appear to be. There will be some disappointments, but you must pick yourself up and move on. To sum it all up, do what makes you happy. Look for where you can find peace and tranquility within. Remember, there is nothing like peace of mind.

A word of caution from me is if you know someone that you have to justify your words when speaking to them—Run. That's a mental case, and you do not want to be involved.

I'm a mental case myself.

So, I should know, right?

Ha! Ha! Ha!

And if you are talking to someone and everything you say, they say they know it, too. Beware! You are talking to a liar.

When I am conversing with people and I know they are using the wrong word and I know the right word, I usually tell them the correct word. This causes friction sometimes.

But now, with everything draining my strength, mentally and medically, I am no longer interested in correcting anyone anymore.

Say whatever you like.

This I find hilarious:

A disabled young lady told me she did not want the preacher to pray for her, so I asked, "Why not?" Then she said, "I might get healed, s**t, my check might get cut off, I need my check." I know it was wrong, but we laughed. And to be honest, I burst out laughing every time I think of it.

This I find too blunt:

Many years ago, my mama and my second oldest sister, went to visit a sick lady and asked her if she would like them to pray for her. She said, "No, y'all might pray for me to die."

LINDA'S PRAYER:

Thank You, **LORD**, for carrying me from then until now, every step of the way.

Oh, **LORD**, I pray, be with me every day.

Thank You, **LORD**, for not leaving me along the way, because You are my stay.

I am lost without You.

In Jesus' name, I pray,

Amen.

"They prevented me in the day of my calamity: but the LORD was my stay."

(Psalms 18:18 KJV)

SICKNESS

I am sick beyond sickness. But by God's grace, I am holding on. My husband keeps saying I need to gain some weight. As, of now, I weigh 121.9 pounds, but as long as I do not go over 127 pounds, I am fine. I have joint pains, and cannot bear carrying around excess weight even though my husband assists me. Also, my TMJ (temporomandibular joint disorder), IBS (irritable bowel syndrome), and IBD (inflammatory bowel disease) will not allow me to eat much. Sometimes, I think he forgets about those things. Truthfully, mostly, I think he is afraid of losing me to these dreadful conditions. He does not even want to converse with me on the subject. Thank God, I have my sister-cousin, a nickname for one of my best friends, and we call each other. I mentioned her earlier; we met back in 1990 when she became my hairdresser. In her, God blessed me with a true and faithful friend, one of my miracles. She has always been my best friend. Always. (BFA).

As usual, I called out to my husband, Sweet Baby, for some Ginger Ale, my go-to drink when I am nauseous. Finally, I drifted off to sleep. After I had awakened again, we started our daily routine.

For weeks now, this new fried chicken place has kept popping up in my email. So, I told Sweet Baby I needed to get out of the house. We went to the new chicken place in Darlington, SC but it was closed. God willing, I will get some chicken, shrimp, and other fixings from there soon. But today I settled for some fried chicken nuggets from another place. Sweet Baby is going to prepare some shrimp and grits later. I know they are going to be delicious.

I rather eat my husband's cooking than anyone else's. He was the Head Chef aboard a submarine in the U.S. Navy. He went to a Class A Naval Certified Chef School by the U.S. Navy, and a Culinary Arts School (Johnson & Wales), where he became a Certified Chef in both institutes.

After returning home, I was so happy to get back in my bed. The rough roads upset my stomach. And I am in unbearable pain. My legs and feet are numb, and painful, too. Neurological conditions have badly messed me up.

But I thank God for life.

Before I met my insurance deductible, I had to pay $400 plus for 30 tablets of one of my medications. Now, those same 30 tablets are costing $600 plus regardless.

I am a U.S. Army Veteran who likes my civilian doctors but something has to give. My husband had tried many years ago, telling me I needed a military identification card (ID), so I could get my medications from the Veterans' hospital. It took me 41 years to decide; I am now ready for that. But sometimes, I get so tired that I do not care about anything medical. I received my U.S. Department of Veterans Affairs Member ID card.

EPILOGUE

During my childhood, I led a sheltered existence. I knew nothing about prescription drugs because my mama and my second oldest sister always had home remedies. And of course, I knew nothing about illicit drugs. But I knew about beer because my fourth oldest brother and one of his friends drank it all the time. They both have passed away; God rest their souls.

Seeing all the hedonistic goings-on after leaving home was shocking for me. My mind went to what would my mama and second oldest sister think. At first, I resisted the temptation of smoking, drinking, etc. But after a while, I strayed from my religious upbringing. But hallelujah, I've returned! I have learned with Jesus Christ on my side, I can do all things. He gives me the strength.

Many years ago, I decided to be who I am. I told my hairdresser, the same one that I have to this very day, to not worry about my scars showing. She was shocked, and could not believe that I did not care anymore. When I look at a black-and-white photo my husband took of me recently, I really noticed for the first time how pronounced my scars are. But instead of wanting to cover them again, I took a Biblical standpoint—you see; I have three scars on my forehead—in the name of the Father, Son, and Holy Spirit (Ghost). Because my mind is mostly on heavenly things now.

When I spoke to my niece on Easter Day, I told her I am sick. I often remember the really great times we had together. She lives in another state now. I saw her recently and a lot more of my nephews and nieces that I had not seen in quite a while. Oh, what a blessing that was. I promised her I would send her some pictures of her, my other niece (Stephanie), and me. We used to be the trio. She is now married, with a beautiful family of her own. And Stephanie has a beautiful family as well.

When I was a girl of 16, I met a young lady and she was very sick and very sad. At the time, I could not understand why. Then, after visiting with her inside of the home, I went outside where her mama was sitting on the porch. I asked her mama, "Why is your daughter so sad?"

Because here I was, young and happy, and so full of life. Just beginning to live.

Then she said to me, "She is tired and wants to go home." Crazy me, I was thinking to myself, she's at home.

I did not understand. Now, I do. She wanted to go to her Heavenly home.

My road is long, difficult, very painful, and paved with suffering. I am in pain every day. My doctor diagnosed me with an inflammatory bowel disease. It has gotten worse over the years.

A few months back, I said to myself, if complications from this inflammatory bowel disease take me out, I am thankful that I am not so young and not so vibrant and not so full of life as I once was. After talking with my niece, I am glad that we were all young, healthy, and fun-loving back then. My nieces are much younger than I am, though.

Some of my family members have really been there for me. More so now than ever. To God, I am thankful. I love my family more than my life. It was not always like that because I was very selfish. But finding the LORD for myself, changed my entire stance about life. I pray each day for God to help me to be a better person.

Especially, a good helpmeet for my husband.

At a dental appointment, while waiting for the hygienist to clean my teeth. On the monitor before me, I saw my teeth and how they had changed. They reminded me of the journey that my life has taken over the years. Some of them were good, others were bad, and some were beyond repair. Also, there was soft rock music playing. I heard a song that I was familiar with while growing up, and a song that I danced to while in the military. Then came Michael Jackson's song "Man In The Mirror." His song made me wonder if I were a better person now than I was back then. I sure pray so.

On May 5, 1990, the most beautiful, sweetest, kindest, meekest, gentlest soul I have ever known was shrouded in burial, my mama. Mother's Day is in a few days, and I have words to say to my church family. Because I am president of the pastor's aide ministry. There are no words to say how sick I am today. There are no parts of my body not untouched by pain. And I have a headache, too. Also, I am so weak and hoarse that I can barely speak.

LORD, please give me the strength to last.

The devil is trying to plant the seed in my head that my departure is at hand; and this I know, but not today. Satan, not today.

I have had problems with my teeth shifting for over a year now. I need extensive dental work done. The dentist started on the left side, and it was very painful. I have TMJ, so that made it even more painful. I had to keep my mouth open wide for long periods of time. The doctor had to keep leaving me and go to other patients because I needed breaks. Two weeks later, I went back for my next appointment on the right side. I was not looking forward to it. But when I went back for the completion of my extensive dental work it was a breeze. It was not as painful and it did not take as long. Of course, my jaw joints were aching, but the doctor did it all at one time with no breaks.

Now, if my stomach would just cooperate, I can eat and drink without having pain in my mouth from my teeth.

My menu has changed again, I am now back to having Sweet Baby season our foods with only salt and pepper because of the worsening of my stomach ailments, irritable bowel syndrome, and inflammatory bowel disease, and my portion sizes are even smaller, believe it or not. But I have been able to maintain my weight beautifully. What a blessing.

Even though my foods are only seasoned with salt and pepper, they are still delicious. My husband knows what to do with food. And he has not once complained about it, although he loves cooking with different seasonings.

I am grateful.

I am now completely homebound, but that is okay, too. Many people may find it troublesome to be inside the house all the time, but not me. Because I do not have the strength or the mind to venture out anymore. I told you in my first book titled *The Day My Life Changed: (An Accident Survivor)*, that I have always been a bit eccentric, but since the accident, it has worsened. Well, that is true now more than ever. By this, I mean I materialize things in my mind. But I am moving on. I have since started a weekly blog and pitched my Healthy Weight Loss Plan on it.

As you recall, I mentioned earlier about getting body-shamed.

But in 2010, because of new medications and supplements, I ballooned to 172 pounds. I was so miserable and disappointed in myself until I had to get the weight off, and I did. And vowed to never let that happen again.

So, now even if I pig out and notice the slightest weight gain, I take care of it right away. Because I have my Healthy Weight Loss Plan to remedy the problem.

In 2011, I weighed 95 pounds. I had never been so small in my life. My wake-up call came one day after my husband had led me into the bathroom and while sitting on the toilet, I almost fell in. I said to myself, *Girl, you better do something.* So, I gradually started gaining my weight back.

Redefining my future yet again, challenging myself further, not giving up, and persevering is difficult. In this book, I am sharing more about my childhood, military life, old boyfriends, first marriage, etc.

This is the path that God had allowed me to choose to get where He intended for me to be today.

Let me say, I wrote most about my husband, Sweet Baby, in my first book.

But here is a little extra, my husband loves me more than I deserve to be loved. I can be so difficult at times, and I always felt like I was not the one to be loved until Sweet Baby showed me that is not true. I know sometimes it is very hard for him to be saddled with me. But I always pray to God to help me to be a good wife. I want to be the best spouse possible. Living in this battled and bruised body, and in this complex state of mind is very tiring.

LORD, help me.

I thank God for giving me the privilege of being associated with Sweet Baby. There is no doubt in my mind that God sent him to me. Our chance meeting was at a time when I needed him most. I am not talking about in a professional way but a spiritual moment. We were thrown together for a brief moment in time that became a lifetime.

The blessings of God are gratuitous, not for something we have done.

For the first time today, I figured out why I love black-and-white movies so much. I love seeing the evolution of the aging of the stars, male and female. Today I saw two of my favorite actors in the same movie. Both of whom I considered handsome when they were younger. But my favorite one of all is Gary Cooper's, "High Noon."

The movie shows how one man had to stand alone, with no help from anyone, but he was brave enough to do what had to be done. And sometimes, that is how I view my life because of all the things that I have been through and all that I am going through.

But I must admit, too, that I love seeing the women in elaborate costumes and the gentlemen dressed so dapper. I learn so much from watching old movies. It is a blessing to be able to grow old gracefully and still look good.

I am thankful that God gives me the mind and the strength to carry on.

There are many things I took for granted when I was younger. I often wish I knew then what knowledge I have now.

I thank God, my weight is holding steady because I still look decent and presentable to others. But for how long? I do not know, because I am at the point where I am wondering, maybe, I should not eat at all. Everything I eat or drink makes me sick to my stomach. But my husband makes homemade lemon-flavored crushed ice that takes away the nauseous feeling for the time being. Remember, I mentioned earlier that Ginger Ale was my go-to drink, so we will see what happens with my sensitive stomach. Sometimes, I get so sick that, I do not think I am going to be too much longer in this life. But of course, I do not know, only God knows.

I pray to God, please help no one else to feel sick like this.

During my childhood, I experienced racism, at that time I did not have anything to comfort my soul, but nowadays, the scent of lavender soap uplifts my spirit. To me, the best way to experience it is when the water is as hot as I can stand it. Because hot water causes the lavender to permeate my senses and it takes me to a place of euphoria. It is like—an addictive drug—I must have it.

I did not know there was such a thing as lavender toilet paper until recently. Now, I do not know whether to sniff it or use it, because I am so addicted to lavender. The scent calms me like nothing else. I have all kinds of lavender products.

My mind is devoid of all nonsense. I am so at peace within, and with the world, even though this inflammatory bowel disease is slowly killing me with all the pains and burning. And on top of all the other medical conditions I am suffering from because of the horrific accident that nearly took my life, and left me totally and permanently disabled.

I would be amiss ending this book, without mentioning my half-sister, who is like a full sister to me. She and her family support me whenever they can. And I need to mention my sister who died in childbirth. I love all of my siblings the same.

My friends, I leave this with you: I have had a good run. First, my Daddy, my Mama, my second oldest sister, and my oldest brother passed the torch.

And this man here, my Sweet Baby, brought me to the finish line.

Then, I crossed over it; when I came back full circle to Jesus Christ, Who is the head of my life.

I am a winner!

I pray that my book will be an enlightenment to someone as they play out their own production of this thing called life.

I pray that my Healthy Weight Loss Plan can help someone achieve their desired weight loss goal. And be successful at maintaining it.

I want my blog to help someone who is struggling daily, like me.

My friends, have you figured it out by now, since I have come back full circle to Jesus Christ, the shelf life for my religion has expired?

Hallelujah!

As I said in my first book numinous, (spiritual) things happened; they happened in this book as well. Again, they had to be God's doings.

I wrote about this in my first book, how the LORD's Holy Spirit leads, guides, and strengthens me always. But I need to say, the spirit is willing but the flesh is weak.

God is my anchor!

I wrote this book about my life, but I just want my name written in the Book of Life.

"And whosoever was not found written in the book of life was cast into the lake of fire."

(Revelation 20:15 KJV)

The Day I Found The LORD (For Myself), *all* of my sins were forgiven.

"If we confess our sins, he is faithful and just to forgive us *our* sins, and to cleanse us from all unrighteousness."

(1 John 1:9 KJV)

I have no regrets!

"No man can justly censure or condemn another, because indeed no man truly knows another." Sir Thomas Browne (Religio Medici)

"I had fainted, unless I had believed to see the goodness of the LORD in the land of the living."

(Psalms 27:13 KJV)

God Bless,

A Soldier in the Army of the LORD

RESOURCES AND REFERENCES

If you are interested in reading my blog, go to: www.lindacrosbyauthor.com.

You can purchase my Healthy Weight Loss Plan by going to my email: lindacrosby@lindacrosbyauthor.com.

Or on my blog and/or make a donation of your choice. It is a secure website and all transactions are private.

If you are not comfortable putting your personal information online, please send $5, along with your email address for my Plan, and/or send a donation of your choice to P.O. Box 1084, Lake City, SC 29560. When I receive your $5, I will email my Healthy Weight Loss Plan to the address that you have provided.

You can purchase my first book titled *The Day My Life Changed: (An Accident Survivor)*, on my blog or send me an email or inquire at the mailing address I have provided. (See all above.)

And you can also go to:

https://bookstore.dorrancepublishing.com/the-day-my-life-changed-an-accident-survivor/. Or www.dorrancebookstore.com.

Or call Dorrance Bookstore at: 1-800-788-7654.

Disclaimer:

Please check with your doctor before trying my Healthy Weight Loss Plan.

Even though it is personally tried and true.

What works for me, may or may not, work for you.

For more copies of The Day I Found The LORD (For Myself), go to: www.readersmagnet.com.

While you are there you can also find my Poetry book: *Sweet Baby (Peace of Mind)*.

And the Audiobook of: *The Day My Life Changed: (An Accident Survivor)*.

www.ingramcontent.com/pod-product-compliance
Lightning Source LLC
LaVergne TN
LVHW010617070526
838199LV00063BA/5173